P9-DWD-830

The Great
Wall of China

GREAT STRUCTURES IN HISTORY

Other titles in this series

The Great Wall of China

GREAT STRUCTURES IN HISTORY

Rachel Lynette

KIDHAVEN PRESS
An imprint of Thomson Gale, a part of The Thomson Corporation

THOMSON
™
GALE

Detroit • New York • San Francisco • San Diego • New Haven, Conn.
Waterville, Maine • London • Munich

For more information, contact
KidHaven Press
27500 Drake Rd.
Farmington Hills, MI 48331-3535
Or you can visit our Internet site at http://www.gale.com

LIBRARY OF CONGRESS CATALOGING-IN-PUBLICATION DATA

Lynette, Rachel, 1964-
 The Great Wall of China / by Rachel Lynette.
  p. cm. — (Great structures in history)
 Includes bibliographical references.
Summary: Discusses the Great Wall of China including why it was built, who built it, how it was constructed, how it was used, its deterioration, and its repair and restoration.
 ISBN 0-7377-1558-8
 1. Great Wall of China (China)—History—Juvenile Literature. [Great Wall of China (China)—History.] I. Title. II. Series.

Printed in the United States of America

CONTENTS

CHAPTER ONE

The Longest Wall on Earth

The Great Wall of China is the longest structure ever built on planet Earth. It is often called the Great Dragon of China because it winds across northern China like a giant snake. The wall begins at China's eastern border in the city of Shanhaiguan. It goes by China's capital city, Beijing, where royalty once lived in the Forbidden City. It twists its way over steep mountain ranges, through frozen plains and across muddy grasslands, and finally comes to an end deep in the Gobi desert.

Through the years the wall has crumbled into rubble and has been rebuilt many times. Its path has changed with each rebuilding. Many smaller walls have been added, branching out from the main one. It took more than two thousand years and millions of people to build the Great Wall. Most of these people were forced to work on the wall, and many of them died on the job. The wall and the land nearby contain the remains of many of these laborers, giving the Great Wall of China another nickname: the Longest Cemetery on Earth.

This section of the 1,850-mile long Great Wall winds through the mountainous area of Hebei Province in northern China.

The Size of the Wall

People have a hard time agreeing exactly how long the Great Wall is. It has been different lengths at different times in history. The main wall is 1,850 miles (2,977 kilometers) long, about the distance from Lake Superior in Michigan to the Atlantic Ocean at the tip of Florida. However, if all of the branches are included, it stretches nearly 4,000 miles (6,437 kilometers), which is the distance from Miami, Florida, all the way to the North Pole.

The wall is not only long, but also wide and tall. It is thicker at the bottom than it is at the top to support its massive weight. At the top the wall ranges from ten to fifteen feet (three to five meters) across. That is wide enough for ten people to walk side by side. It is even wide enough to drive a car on, or in ancient times, for three horses to walk side by side. The wall also varies in height. The tallest sections are nearly thirty feet (nine meters) high, while lower sections are closer to twenty feet (six meters).

The Beauty of the Wall

The size of the wall is not the only thing remarkable about it. It is also beautiful. Many of the architects and builders took great pride in their work, especially those who worked on later walls. All along the wall are examples of excellent workmanship. Elaborate carvings, often signed, can be found on towers, gates, and on the wall itself. Arched doorways and windows add to the beauty. These details, as well as the uniform design of the wall as it twists and curves across the Chinese landscape, make it an awe-inspiring sight.

Because it was used to defend China from its enemies, the wall was home to millions of soldiers and was used as a storehouse for weapons and supplies. Buildings and other architectural features were built on and along the wall to aid soldiers in defending their homeland.

Although the wall's primary purpose was to protect China from its enemies, it also served to isolate China from the influences of other cultures for thousands of years. The ancient Chinese people considered China to be the center of the universe because they were so advanced artistically and culturally. They thought of themselves as the only civilized people and believed all other people to be inferior and not worthy of Chinese culture. The Great Wall kept China apart from the rest of the world for many years, and Chinese culture flourished.

Although the Chinese were unified in their desire to keep foreigners out of China, they were not always at peace with each other. For hundreds of years the Chinese fought within their own borders.

Wall Building in China

From 481 to 221 B.C., a time in Chinese history known as the warring states period, the land was divided into small kingdoms or states. The rulers of these kingdoms wanted to acquire more land. They were constantly at war with their neighbors, either trying to get others' land or protecting their own. In addition, nomadic tribes often attacked states on China's northern border. These tribes, traveling on horseback, would raid Chinese villages. They would steal food, kill villagers, and burn down houses. States, and sometimes even villages, built long walls to protect themselves from their enemies.

By the end of the warring states period, there were hundreds of miles of walls all over China. This period ended when the ruler of the state of Qin, a boy of fourteen named Zheng, rose to power. Zheng's armies fought bloody battles for nearly twenty years. He

The top of the wall is wide enough to allow three horses or ten people to walk side by side.

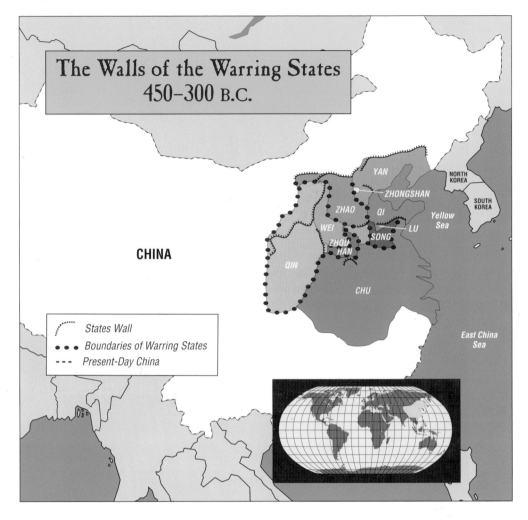

The Walls of the Warring States 450–300 B.C.

YAN

ZHONGSHAN

NORTH KOREA

SOUTH KOREA

ZHAO

QI

Yellow Sea

WEI

LU

ZHOU
HAN

SONG

CHINA

QIN

CHU

East China Sea

Legend:
····· States Wall
●●● Boundaries of Warring States
--- Present-Day China

conquered the other states in China, creating one unified country. Zheng called himself Qin, the first sovereign emperor of China.

The First Great Wall

Qin had all the walls that divided the newly conquered states torn down, but he left the walls along China's northern border. He decided to connect these walls to build one long wall to protect the newly unified China against its enemies in the north. This was to be the first Great Wall.

Qin knew that building the wall would be a huge job. It would require thousands of workers and massive amounts of building materials. In addition, he would have to supply his workers with food, living quarters, tools, and other necessary items. The wall would also have to be carefully designed to keep China's enemies out. Qin chose Meng T'ien, one of his most trusted military leaders, to oversee its building.

CHAPTER TWO

Building and Rebuilding the Wall

T'ien planned the route of the wall carefully. He took advantage of the walls already in existence. They were repaired and new walls were built connecting them. Most of the wall was built using an ancient building method called **hang-tu**. *Hang* means "pounded" and *tu* means "earth." So *hang-tu* can be translated as "pounded earth."

Building the Wall

For each section of the wall, a form or frame was built out of wood or bamboo. Next, a layer of dirt was poured into the form. Workers would stand on the dirt and use simple pounding tools to beat the earth down inside the form. Then another layer of dirt could be added and pounded. Each layer was only a few inches thick, so it took many layers to make a wall. When the wall was the right height, the forms were taken away. Although slow, this method made a strong wall.

The workers had few tools. Some had shovels, but most workers dug the dirt by hand. The dirt was loaded into baskets to be carried to the wall by others. Workers used whatever materials they could find to build the wall. Soil, stones, sand, and sticks all went into the forms. Ladders were made by lashing pieces of bamboo together. When wood or bamboo could not be found nearby to make the forms, it was brought in from other places, sometimes from more than one hundred miles away.

Using the hang-tu method, workers fill a wooden mold with dirt while other workers use pounding tools to pack the layers of earth. When the frame is removed, a tightly packed earth wall remains.

Lives of the Workers

The workers came from all walks of life. Peasants were taken from their land. Convicts were taken from prison and forced to work in chains. Merchants, teachers, doctors, and other members of China's upper classes were forced into labor by Qin's soldiers. When there were no more men, women were forced into labor. Small children were left to fend for themselves while their mothers toiled on the wall.

Life along the wall was extremely difficult. Workers labored for long hours in severe weather conditions. In

Some of the workers on the Great Wall had to work in the mountains where there are frequent snowstorms and the temperature drops to twenty degrees.

the deserts the temperatures could reach more than one hundred degrees Fahrenheit (thirty-eight degrees Celsius). In the mountains workers endured frequent snowstorms and temperatures below twenty degrees Fahrenheit (negative seven degrees Celsius). Workers were fed barely enough to stay alive because there was not much food to give them. Most farmers were working on the wall so there were not enough people left on the farms to tend the fields or harvest crops. Bandits often stole what little food there was before it got to the workers. Workers slept in poorly constructed camps near the wall. Their shelters did not keep out the cold and rain, and workers did not have blankets. Often there was not enough room for everyone in the shelters, so many slept outside on the ground. Workers were not given clothes, and many wore rags or animal skins. In summer they wore nothing at all.

A Reminder of Cruelty

No one knows how many people died working on the wall, but historians believe it was close to a million. They died of hunger, disease, and exposure. Many were killed by the soldiers who guarded them. Although some may have been buried in the wall itself, the majority of the dead were thrown into large trenches dug beside the wall. T'ien was able to build the wall in only seven years, but when the wall was complete it was a reminder of the cruelty of the first emperor, rather than a symbol of unified China as Qin had planned.

The wall was completed in 207 B.C. It was more than 2,500 miles (4,020 kilometers) long. Qin died just three years later. As custom required, T'ien committed suicide shortly thereafter.

China was ruled by several different dynasties over the next fifteen hundred years. Some of these rulers let the wall fall into disrepair. Others rebuilt it, sometimes extending its length. When the Ming dynasty came into power in A.D. 1368, the wall was in poor condition. But during a period of two hundred years the Ming dynasty rebuilt the wall, making it bigger and grander than ever before.

The Ming Wall

Like the builders of earlier walls, the Ming builders used materials they could find near the building site. But they also brought in materials from other locations. Timber was cut into planks and transported from the forests in the north. Stones were taken from quarries miles away. Some of these building materials were carried to the wall by donkeys and goats, or in carts. Most of the building materials, though, were transported on the backs of peasants. Peasants often traveled for many miles with their heavy loads. Sometimes hundreds of workers formed a line and passed the stones from hand to hand. This worked especially well on steep terrain. These "human conveyor belts" could be miles long.

Ming builders used more advanced techniques than the builders of earlier walls. The most important of these was the use of bricks. Although bricks had some-

Emperor Qin, enjoying a promenade in a *palinquin*, decided to build the Great Wall to protect China from its enemies in the north.

times been used in earlier walls, Ming builders improved the brick-making process. The bricks for the Ming Wall were made as close to the building site as possible. They were made of clay, which was packed into wooden molds so that all of the bricks would be the same size. After they dried, the bricks were removed

Ming laborers mold bricks and then harden them by baking them in a kiln for many hours at high temperatures.

from the molds and baked for many hours in dome-shaped **kilns**. The kilns were made of rocks and were heated with fires to very high temperatures. When the bricks cooled they were as hard as the kiln rocks. Then they were ready to use on the wall.

Rather than using temporary frames made from wood, Ming builders built outer edges of the wall using several layers of bricks. The inside was then filled with dirt and debris, and was packed down. Finally a layer of bricks was added to the top of the wall. This method created a stronger wall. It also made it possible to build in the mountains and on other steep terrain. Parts of the Ming Wall are built on narrow ridges and cliff edges. This would not have been possible without the use of bricks.

In some sections quarried granite was used for the base of the wall rather than bricks. It had to be cut to the right shape and size by skilled stonecutters. Granite is a very hard stone. It made the wall strong, but it was difficult to cut and heavy to carry.

Other advanced building techniques included the use of simple machines. Ropes and pulleys were used to move baskets of building materials to the top of the wall. The Ming workers also installed drains that allowed rainwater to flow off the wall. In the past, puddles had caused the wall to erode. Draining the water made the wall much more stable.

The use of bricks made it possible to build the Great Wall in the mountains and on other steep terrain.

Ming workers build the outer edges of the wall with bricks and then use a crank-driven system to lift dirt and stones to fill the inside of the wall.

The Ming builders did excellent work, and the wall was an effective barrier against China's enemies for many years. The Ming Wall was the last Great Wall, ending a tradition that had been a part of Chinese culture since the first emperor, Qin.

CHAPTER THREE

A Wall with a Purpose

When Qin came into power most of the Chinese people were farmers. They lived in villages and worked their small patches of land. The land to the north was dry and did not make good farmland. The people who lived on this land were called the Xiongnu. They were nomads, moving from place to place with their herds of goats and yaks. The Xiongnu frequently raided Chinese villages. They stole food, killed peasants, and burned buildings.

Qin's wall stopped these attacks. The Xiongnu did not attempt to fight the soldiers stationed along the wall. Most were so frightened by the size and grandeur of the wall that they would not even graze their animals within sight of it. Qin succeeded in protecting his people, but for a while there were few of them to protect. Most of the people had died working on the wall. Those remaining were angry and resentful rather than grateful.

Protecting Traders

From 605 B.C. to about A.D. 186 the wall was used to protect trading caravans as they traveled along the Silk

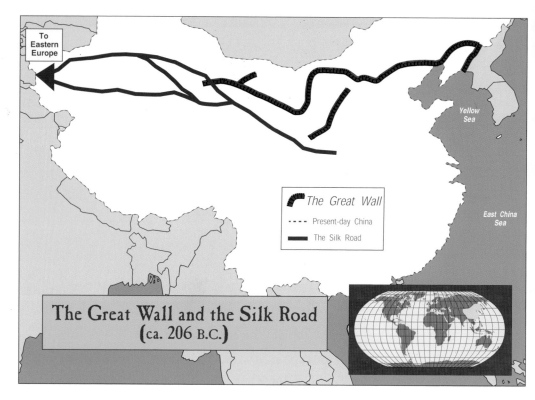

The Great Wall and the Silk Road
(ca. 206 B.C.)

Road. The Silk Road was a trade route that stretched through northern China into the Middle East and ended in eastern Europe. Although the Chinese considered themselves superior to all other cultures, they realized that other Asian people, Arabs, and Europeans wanted things they had. Silk, tea, paper, spices, jade, and many other items all found eager buyers in far-off lands. Meanwhile goods from Europe found buyers in China. Even their old enemy, the Xiongnu, traded with China. During this time, hundreds of miles were added to the western end of the wall to protect the Silk Road. Soldiers on the wall kept caravans safe from thieves and guarded border crossings into China.

Although the Chinese no longer feared attack from the Xiongnu, new enemies began to invade from the north. Under the rule of a series of dynasties, Chinese armies fought various tribes, often extending and reinforcing the wall. Eventually China's territory extended into the north beyond the wall. This made the wall useless as a military defense since it was no longer positioned on the border. The wall was neglected for many years. By the time the Mongols, led by Genghis Khan, attacked in 1215 the wall could not keep them out. The Mongols ruled for 150 years. After years of fighting, in 1368 they were overthrown. The Ming dynasty then came into power.

Defending China from the Mongols

Although the Mongols had been conquered and forced out of China, they were still a serious threat.

This part of the Great Wall near Badaling prevented enemies from the north from invading the capital through Juyongguan Pass.

Rulers of the Ming dynasty did not want to lose their country to the Mongols again. The wall once again became important for China's defense.

The rebuilding of the wall began with the first Ming ruler, Hung-wu. By this time most of the old wall had been reduced to rubble. Although all the Ming rulers worked on the wall, it was the thirteenth Ming ruler, Wan-li, who did the most work. One of the names for the Great Wall is Wan-li's Long Wall. The new wall was built just south of previous walls. The Ming included many of the same features of the walls that came before, but they improved on them. These features were built into the wall to help the soldiers defend it.

These watchtowers at Badaling are a few of the twenty-five thousand watchtowers that were spaced six hundred feet apart along the entire length of the wall.

The Design of the Wall

More than twenty-five thousand **watchtowers**, sometimes called ramparts, were built along the wall. These towers varied in size. The larger ones extended several feet beyond the sides of the wall and were called block-houses. The more common, smaller towers were the same width as the wall and were two or three stories high. The lower levels were used to store weapons and supplies, and to house some of the soldiers. Soldiers used the top story to keep watch and to defend the wall from enemies. Watchtowers were spaced 600 feet (182.9 meters) apart. Because a soldier could shoot an arrow just over 300 feet (91.4 meters), any enemy who scaled the wall would be within bow range of one of the towers.

Buttresses were structures that stuck out from the wall on the northern side. Unlike towers, they did not rise above the wall. They helped to support it and served as supply rooms. They also made it easier for soldiers to see and shoot their enemies. From the buttresses soldiers had clear shots at enemies approaching the wall. They could also shoot at the backs of enemies who were trying to scale the wall.

The wall also included many gates. These were necessary so that soldiers and ordinary citizens could cross easily from one side of the wall to the other. These gates were usually made from wood and were heavily guarded. Larger gates, called **passes**, were located at strategic points. Passes included large,

The rectangular crenels in the side of this wall allowed soldiers to shoot arrows at the enemy while staying hidden from view.

castlelike structures and were topped by tall towers. The gates themselves were built into arches and were secured with iron bolts.

In addition to these large features, there were also some smaller ones that were important in defending China. The top of the wall was spanned on both edges by three-foot walls called **parapets**. These small walls provided protection for the Chinese soldiers during attacks and prevented people from falling off the wall. In many places small, rectangular holes called **crenels** were cut into the parapets, watchtowers, and buttresses. Crenels allowed the soldiers to shoot arrows at the enemy while staying protected.

Most of the soldiers lived in **garrisons** along the wall. A garrison could house anywhere from a few hundred to a few thousand soldiers, depending on its strategic location. These consisted of large buildings that included barracks for soldiers, horse stables, and supply rooms.

Each garrison also included a **signal beacon**. Like the garrisons, these tall towers, sometimes called kiosks or mounds, were built near the wall, not on it. Often they were built on hilltops so they could be seen from a great distance. Signal beacons were used as lookout towers and to send smoke or fire signals along the length of the wall.

Soldiers Along the Wall

The main duty of soldiers along the wall was to patrol its length looking for enemies. When an enemy was spotted,

A stone statue shows a Ming warrior with his weapons and armor protecting the Great Wall and China from enemy Mongols.

soldiers sent signals from the beacon towers to alert the other soldiers on the wall. The Ming dynasty had an elaborate system of signals. Soldiers during this period, like those who guarded earlier walls, signaled with smoke during the day and fire at night. With the invention of gunpowder, they also used rockets. The number of fires lit and rockets launched depended on how many enemy soldiers had been spotted. If there were fewer than one hundred enemy soldiers approaching, then only one fire was to be lit. Five fires indicated an attack of more than ten thousand enemy soldiers! When the guards saw a signal from a neighboring beacon, they lit their own signal fires to send the same message farther along the wall. In this way soldiers on other parts of the wall could get ready for attack or send reinforcements.

Soldiers along the wall had a wide variety of weapons to choose from. They used swords, lances, battle-axes, and crossbows. They had metal and wooden shields and were suited in armor made from thick leather.

The Ming soldiers were fierce warriors. For nearly three hundred years they kept the Mongols out of China and kept the wall in excellent repair. China was secure and prosperous until 1620, when Wan-li lost control of his country and in doing so, lost the wall as well.

CHAPTER FOUR

The Great Wall, Still Great Today

For the next three hundred years the Great Wall was neglected. China went through several rebellions and changes in leadership. Finally, in 1949 the **Communist Party**, led by Mao Tse-tung, won the battle to govern the country. By this time what was left of the wall was useless as a barrier to defend China. Even if it were rebuilt, the wall would offer no protection against airplanes, missiles, and other modern weapons. Under the new Communist government, it was thought to be a useless reminder of the past. It was ignored until the 1960s when Mao began the Cultural Revolution.

Bring Down the Wall

Mao launched the Cultural Revolution in 1966. His purpose was to unite the people of China under the Communist government. Mao did not believe that the old ways of China could coexist with the new ones. He wanted to destroy all remnants of ancient Chinese

As part of the Cultural Revolution, Mao had the Communists destroy hundreds of miles of the Great Wall.

culture. Priceless works of art were destroyed, rare books were burned, temples and shrines were ruined, and scholars were killed. The Communists considered the Great Wall to be a symbol of the oppression that common people had suffered under the dynasties of the past. They wanted it completely destroyed. They used dynamite, bulldozers, and huge crews of workers to tear down large sections of the wall. Chinese citizens took parts of it to make their own houses and other buildings. Although the Communists turned hundreds of miles of the wall into rubble, they did not succeed in destroying the whole thing before Mao died and a new leader took control of the country.

Restore the Wall

By 1984 Deng Xiaoping had become the leader of the Communist Party in China. Unlike Mao, he loved the Great Wall and ordered it to be rebuilt and repaired. Almost immediately crews of workers began to restore the wall. Donations for the restoration came from within China and from twenty-six other countries. This money has been used to rebuild parts of the Great Wall and to preserve parts of the original Ming Wall. In addition, some of the donated funds have been used to build the Great Wall Museum in Badaling. Badaling is located in the mountains just forty miles from Beijing. Also at Badaling is a large monument inscribed with Deng Xiaoping's famous words, "Love Our Motherland and Rebuild the Great Wall."

The wall is not only an important part of Chinese history, but it is also one of the greatest structures on the planet. In 1987 the Great Wall of China was made an official World Heritage site by the United Nations

When Deng Xiaoping became the leader of Communist China in 1984, he began to rebuild and repair the Great Wall.

Educational, Scientific and Cultural Organization (UNESCO). This means that, like Stonehenge in Great Britain and the Taj Mahal in India, the Great Wall is now considered one of the world's most important structures. The work that began in the 1980s to rebuild the wall continues today.

Workers continue the restoration work that was begun in the 1980s, but less than 30 percent of the wall is in good condition.

Restoration Challenges

Rebuilding the wall is a challenging task for many reasons. Even to rebuild a small section requires a great deal of money and many workers. The method of rebuilding has also become a challenge. Today we have machinery and technology that was not available to the ancient Chinese. But many people think the wall should be constructed using only methods and materials used on the Ming Wall. Others want to use more modern methods. Different groups have taken on rebuilding different sections of the wall. Since there is no single organization or agency in charge of rebuilding the wall, each group does what it wants.

Different Goals

Some restoration projects are sponsored by the government or by organizations that want to preserve the wall as a historic monument. These groups will often copy the ancient architecture, sometimes even using the same construction methods. Sometimes a small village will decide to repair or rebuild the section of the wall that runs nearby using whatever materials are at hand. But most of the rebuilding has been done by businesses that want to make money from tourists who come to see the wall. These people often care more about making their section of the wall appealing and accessible to tourists than in preserving parts of the original Ming Wall.

The Wall Today

The Great Wall today is not a long, uniform wall, but rather a series of disconnected sections. While some sections are maintained and kept in good condition, most are not. In December 2002 the China Great Wall Academy did a survey of 101 sections of the wall throughout northern China. They found that less than 30 percent of the wall was in good condition. The rest had suffered damage from both nature and people.

Nature has been especially hard on the eastern end of the wall. This area is mostly desert. The wind has eroded parts of the wall and sandstorms have left many sections buried. Other parts have been damaged by rain and snow. But people have had a far more damaging effect.

Tourism and the Wall

Tourism is a big part of China's economy, and the Great Wall of China is by far China's biggest tourist attraction. Millions of foreign tourists come to the wall each year. Many tourists from within China also come to see the great monument. Unfortunately, all of those people have had a damaging effect on the wall. Most people want to walk on the wall. Many want to visit the hard-to-reach sections that hug mountain peaks and cliffs. Tourists are not always considerate visitors. Many leave trash behind or try to pry off small sections of the wall as souvenirs.

Finding a Balance

Rather than encouraging visitors to learn about the wall and treat it in a respectful manner, business owners have made many parts of it into tourist traps.

These people are among the millions of foreigners who visit China's biggest tourist attraction every year.

Gift shops selling cheap souvenirs can be found everywhere. Billboards, water parks, bungee jumping facilities, bumper cars, boat rides, cable lifts, and even a horse racetrack have all been built nearby to attract tourists. Since a different business or organization runs each part of the wall, tourists are charged an admission fee for each section they visit.

Although China has benefited economically from the tourists who visit the Great Wall, most people realize a balance must be found between allowing people to enjoy the wall as a tourist attraction and preserving it as an important monument. Many groups continue to work to preserve existing sections and to rebuild other parts in the Ming architectural style. It is unlikely that the Great Wall will ever be completely rebuilt again. But it will forever remain an important part of China's history and an enduring symbol of pride for the Chinese people.

Glossary

buttress: A solid structure, usually made of brick or stone, that is built against a wall to support it.

Communist Party: A political group that believes in a society without different classes. Farms and factories are owned and controlled by all its members. Everyone works for the good of the country, rather than for individual gain.

crenel: A small, rectangular opening in the top of a castle, wall, or parapet.

garrison: A military stronghold where soldiers are housed.

hang-tu: Translated as "pounded earth." An ancient method for constructing walls in which dirt is pounded in layers within temporary wooden or bamboo frames.

kiln: A furnace or oven that can be heated to very high temperatures for burning, baking, or drying something.

parapet: A low protective wall along the edge of a raised structure.

pass: A large gate built into the wall.

signal beacon: A tower used to send fire or smoke signals.

watchtower: A tower used by soldiers to keep watch for enemies.

For Further Reading

Books

Lesley A. DuTemple, *The Great Wall of China*. Minneapolis: Lerner, 2003. This book covers the history of the wall including information about the dynasties and how the wall was constructed. There are wonderful illustrations and photographs as well as maps and a time line.

Peggy Ferroa and Elaine Chan, *China*. Tarrytown, NY: Benchmark Books, 2000. This book provides a wealth of information on China. It includes chapters on history, geography, government, and culture. Includes colorful photographs, several maps, a time line, and a glossary.

Leonard Everett Fisher, *The Great Wall of China*. New York: Macmillan, 1986. For younger children, this book tells the story of the wall built by the first emperor of China. The story is illustrated by the author and includes Chinese characters on each page, with translations at the back of the book.

Elizabeth Mann, *The Great Wall of China*. New York: Mikaya Press, 1997. This beautifully illustrated book explains in a story format the reasons for building the wall and how it was built. It includes a foldout page showing how an enemy attack on the wall might have looked. Also included are a time line and maps.

Tim McNeese, *The Great Wall of China.* San Diego, CA: Lucent Books, 1997. This book tells about the history of the wall including details about the reasons it was built, construction methods, and architectural features. There are also interesting sidebars and a time line.

Web Sites

Dim Sum: The Great Wall of China Photographs (www.newton.mec.edu). A wonderful collection of photographs of the Great Wall, with a link to background information.

Travel China Guide (www.travelchinaguide.com). This site provides links to information about the wall including its history and construction. There are also links to photographs of the wall and information about other tourist attractions in China.

Walk the Great Wall (www.walkthewall.com). This site allows visitors to "walk" the wall by using a mouse to look over 360 degrees of scenery along the wall. The site gives a little information about the scenes. The photographs are black and white, but still quite vivid.

Index

Picture Credits

Cover image: Chinese National Tourist Office
© Dean Conger/CORBIS, 25, 30, 36
Corel, 11 (inset)
© Bennett Dean; Eye Ubiquitous/CORBIS, 28
© Ric Ergenbright/CORBIS, 26–27
Giraudon/Art Resource, NY, 19
© Werner Forman/CORBIS, 21
© Dallas and John Heaton/CORBIS, 35
Chris Jouan, 15
© Melvyn P. Lawes; Papilio/CORBIS, 39
© Liu Liqun/CORBIS, 16
Photodisc, 7
Photos.com, 27 (inset)
Snark/Art Resource, NY, 33
© Keren Su/CORBIS, 11

About the Author

Rachel Lynette has written four other books for KidHaven Press, as well as dozens of articles on children and family life. She has taught children of all ages and is currently working as a technology teacher in Seattle, Washington. Lynette lives in the Songaia Cohousing Community with her husband, Scott; her two children, David and Lucy; a cat named Cookie; and two playful rats. When she is not teaching or writing, she enjoys spending time with her family and friends, reading, drawing, biking, and rollerblading.